269 *Amazing* SEX TIPS & TRICKS FOR HER

ANNE HOOPER

PHILLIP HODSON

SOURCEBOOKS CASABLANCA™
AN IMPRINT OF SOURCEBOOKS, INC.®
NAPERVILLE, ILLINOIS

First published in Great Britain in 2001 by Robson Books, The Chrysalis Building,
Bramley Road, London W10 6SP, a member of the Chrysalis BooksGroup. © 2001 Anne
Hooper and Phillip Hodson

Published by Sourcebooks Casablanca, an imprint of Sourcebooks, Inc.
P.O. Box 4410, Naperville, Illinois 60567-4410
(630) 961-3900
Fax: (630) 961-2168
www.sourcebooks.com
Library of Congress Cataloging-in-Publication Data

Hooper, Anne
  269 amazing sex tips and tricks for her / by Anne Hooper and Phillip Hodson.
    p. cm.
  Rev. ed. of: 269 amazing sex tips and tricks for women. c2003.
  Includes bibliographical references and index.
  1. Sex instruction for women. 2. Women--Sexual behavior. 3. Sexual excitement. I.
Hodson, Phillip. II. Hooper, Anne- 269 amazing sex tips and tricks for women. III. Title.
IV. Title: Two hundred and sixty-nine amazing sex tips and tricks for her.
  HQ46.H76 2009
  613.9'6082--dc22

                                    200903071

                        Printed and bound in the United States of America.
                        SP 10 9 8 7 6 5 4 3 2 1

CONTENTS

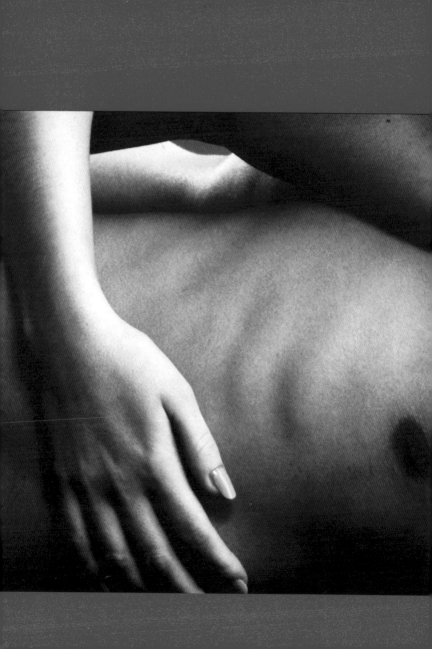

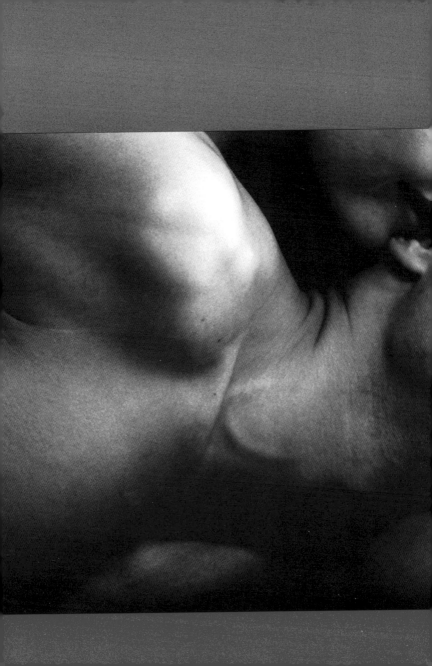

one | MIND JOY

feel good
ABOUT YOURSELF

1   It is easy to create an intimate relationship with someone when you respect and like yourself.

Believe that you are:

○ Attractive

○ Interesting

○ Sexy

○ Loving

2   If you have any doubts, go for assertion training, which will help you feel great.

live IN THE MOMENT

3 The sex that blew the top of your head off yesterday was yesterday. Make each day, each lovemaking session, new.

4 See erotic fantasy as a gorgeous, life-enhancing pleasure in itself. Don't look at it as a means to an end.

FANTASIZE

Sexual fantasy is a unique sexual experience, since it embodies a type of tension that can't be really experienced in the flesh. This tension is also the erotic pull between what may be wonderful for you but bad for others. It represents the balance between freedom of thought and repression of the forbidden.

The top five female fantasies:

5 Swimming in a sunlit sea where the ripples of the water and the lapping of the waves induce blissful sensations.

6 The audition where young men are made to show off their bodies as they compete for a starring role.

7 Under the doctor, where the doctor takes advantage while giving a routine examination.

8 Riding with the Hell's Angels—a night of initiation.

9 In the gym—a lesbian fantasy that takes place in the locker room.

surprising MOMENTS

When you get used to a sexual routine, what was once new knowledge shifts from one side of the brain into a kind of dull filing area section on the other side. This filing section lets you now function on automatic pilot instead of carefully thinking everything through every time. This means that if you and your partner want to recapture the freshness of sex, you need to work on the **ELEMENT** of **SURPRISE.**

10 Set up his screen saver with a series of erotic pictures of yourself. (Make sure the photos are ones you wouldn't mind transmitted to the ends of the earth via the Internet.)

11 Leave a suggestive message on his voicemail.

12 Plant a love note in the cereal box.

13 Do something in bed you have never done before.

SHARPEN YOUR
erotic senses BY:

14. Closing your eyes.

15. Touching yourself.

16. Touching your partner but experiencing the touch as pleasure for yourself.

17. Identifying and describing the effects of his touch.

18 Try to see your partner as a person and not just as a fantasy figure. This is important when making a sensual relationship but hard to do since we all suffer from the Distorted Mirror effect when we fall in love. We cannot help but see the lover as someone incredibly enhanced.

You might:

19 Look behind your partner's physical face or body and see through to his sexual self.

20 Close your eyes and breathe in your partner's scent. Try the test of imagining he is part of a line-up and you must identify him, while blindfolded, only by his scent.

21 Think of him and not you. This means from time to time freeing your mind of what you might like to happen to you and truly focusing on what your lover would prefer.

forget YOUR OWN
REWARD

22 Do something for your lover with no thought of yourself. An altruistic approach is wonderful so long as you sense it is reciprocated. Do not, however, fall into the trap of letting him take you for granted.

23 Practice scrupulous dental hygiene. The mouth is the first approach point—give him a treat!

24 When making love, focus on the immediate sensation, and enjoy your sensuality wherever you experience it in your body. Picture an internal flowchart of wonderful circular sensuality.

Let go of the idea of orgasm as your aim. You can get a more extraordinary and extreme body sensation over a long period of time by forgetting about orgasm than you can by aiming specifically at it and seeking a quick release.

IDENTIFY YOUR
sexual flash points

25 A sexual flash point can be a thought: for example, the knowledge that the minute you meet someone special, you want to go to bed with him.

26 Or an urgent desire for sex: women have two special times in their menstrual cycle when this is highly likely to happen. The first is around ovulation—roughly halfway through the menstrual month, and the second is the day before or a couple of days before your period is expected.

27 Observe the seasons. Make the most of spring and autumn. These are the sexiest times of the year.

28 Whatever your flash point may be, once you know it, let yourself enjoy it. Follow it up. Don't resist!

According to the Hite Report for Women, around 30 percent of women can climax regularly through sexual intercourse alone, but around 80 percent can manage it regularly through masturbation.

According to the Kinsey Institute, only 23 percent of younger women regularly experience orgasm, but by the time they get past the age of thirty, around 90 percent of them do.

More interesting statistics:

○ The average female orgasm lasts twenty-one seconds longer than the average male's. (And still women don't get equal pay.)

○ A small survey showed that out of 12 percent of women who had yet to experience orgasm, 6 percent of them managed to do so after training classes.

○ Women discover masturbation at a later age than men.

○ On the other hand, 3 percent of women can fantasize to orgasm.

- Between 10 and 20 percent of women report having an orgasm in their sleep.

- Four percent of females have had a sexual experience with another female in the past 12 months.

- Eleven percent of women have had a same-sex sexual experience in their lifetime.

- Three percent of women have had sex with both males and females in the last 12 months.

- Lesbians are the least promiscuous group of all humans.

- Lesbians spend literally hours more on each other's bodies during lovemaking compared to heterosexuals.

Do not worry if you find yourself equally attracted to women as you are to men. U.S. sex researchers Masters and Johnson found that there is a group of men and women who are genuinely attracted to either sex and that these individuals find it normal and natural to fall in love with either men or women. Bisexuality is not abnormal.

29 Women are one hundred times more likely to be affected by sexual smell than men. Men, on the other hand, react more negatively to strong perfumes. Trick here: lay off the scent yourself, but encourage your man to wear it!

30 On the other hand, men are statistically more likely to be turned on by what they see, by the visual impact of long legs and high heels, the slick of shiny tight trousers, the curve of a rounded bottom. Trick: women could learn from this by training themselves to notice the sexier points about their man. Men's buttocks are one of women's first focal points!

31 To get the most out of sex, you need to give yourself permission to luxuriate in physical pleasure. One woman did so by telling herself that she was a princess and as such was entitled to enjoy any luxury or spoiling that she was offered.

two

TRICKS AND TEMPTATIONS FOR HIM

MOVES

32 Tell your man that you have discovered some new sex tricks that feel great to you, and so that he can get an idea of how sensational they are, you are going to try out their equivalent on him. Then demonstrate. This way you can give him a treat.

33 Find out how similar or different your erogenous zones are.

34 Teach him, through his own experience, what he might do for you.

35 Anti-shyness tip: if your treat consists of oral sex and you feel shy about doing this to him, spread a little ice cream onto his genitals and then lick it off. You like ice cream. You begin with a pleasure. What starts off as a game can turn into a complete feast.

GIVE HIM
THE *three degrees* OF *kissing*

DON'T:

36 Leap straight down his throat with your tongue—he could suffocate!

37 Smear his face with drool.

38 Breathe pure garlic.

39 Be in a tremendous hurry. Slow is not only sexier, it means you don't seem so needy.

DO:

40 Kiss him on the lips softly…

41 Then firmly and…

42 (Not until he is clearly responding), go for HARD.

43 Kiss him on other places such as behind the ears, in and around the ears, and generally nibble around the sides of his neck.

44 Dynamite. Only when he gets really passionate, bite his lip—not too hard, but just enough to give him a jolt.

EAT
sweets

45 The right smell is an aphrodisiac—literally—so work on your diet and on your personal hygiene.

46 Eat pleasant, exotic tastes such as cinnamon, cardamom, peppermint, or lemon for sexy nights in.

47 Avoid garlic, onions, and cheese.

48 Not only does your breath need to smell sweet, but so does your body. What you eat gets exuded through the pores of your skin, and even if you are unaware, you DO smell of your diet. What's more, when your man works his way down to your genitals, the taste he encounters will be influenced by your recent meals...think about it!

49 However, don't wash too much. Your natural body odor is also an aphrodisiac. Remember Emperor Napoleon, who wrote to Empress Josephine to say, "Home in three days—don't wash!"

GROOM
HIS *genitals*

50 The experience of having someone trim and shape the hair around his most private parts is deliciously erotic. There's something about the cold tingle of steel and the brushing of casual fingers around his most sensitive parts that gets the imagination—not to mention the erection—up.

51 Tell him that you are going to transform his appearance. When you are done, his penis will look longer! He probably won't object. You manage this by clipping the pubic hair above his penis so that a diamond-shaped space (pointing upwards) appears above his penis. Then go for the sides of his pubes, trimming these so that they are wide at the top and narrow at the bottom where they meet the scrotum. The difference is startling.

52 The inner nerves. Feel for the space underneath the penis head, at the end of the frenulum, and press. This point is dynamite.

53 The coronal ridge. This ring-like ridge around the head of the penis is packed with nerve endings, and some men can get off from stimulation of this area alone.

54 The perineum. This area of skin between the root of the penis and the anus is so much more sensitive than most people expect that you can orchestrate the entire excitement/ orgasm sequence from here alone. You can begin arousing him by softly stroking this area.

55 You can rotate the pads of your fingers on the areas nearest the penis root and nearest the anal opening to build excitement.

56 And if he promises to come far too quickly, you can block his orgasm by pressing very hard with your finger on the point halfway along the perineum, between the anus and the scrotum. If you press hard and firmly enough, you literally block the ejaculate and prevent orgasm, and your man is then free to carry on with his work in your good cause.

57 A reason many women are nervous about taking the initiative with their men is that they don't really know what they are supposed to be doing. We rehearse for practically every other situation, and there is absolutely no reason why sex should be an exception. Find yourself a small cucumber or a large zucchini, scrub off all traces of pesticides, and begin.

58 Gently slide your lips over the cucumber. Ensure that your teeth do not take a casual bite by wrapping your lips over them as you go down on the little green fellow. You can let your lips relax on the upward move but re-wrap next time you go down. Practice a soft slide, a firm slide, then a downright mouth clamp.

59 Try taking the cucumber into the front of your mouth, then the back of the mouth; experiment with how much of it you can comfortably suck on before becoming unable to breathe. Let the saliva flow freely.

60 Special trick: as you slide backward and forward, practice flicking the underneath of the cucumber head with your pointed tongue. If this were a real penis, your tongue would catch on the frenulum.

massage TRICKS

All massages need to start off with an all-over body massage. But sooner or later, your man is going to nudge you in the direction between his legs. Here's how you can offer your lover an amazing experience.

61 Holding his penis with your left hand, place your right palm across the head. After every up and down of the left hand, circle the right hand lightly on the head. As the bottom hand goes down, you bring the top hand up. Next you take the top hand down at the same time as you bring the bottom hand up. These two moves constitute the main stroke.

62 The twist. Same as the previous stroke, only you twist each hand slightly.

63 The double ring. Ring his penis with your thumb and forefinger and use the rings to firmly run up and down his penis, first together in the same direction, then apart. Then round and back while still moving up and down. Finally round and back while moving in opposite directions.

condom TRICKS

64 Hold the condom in one hand, by the tip, squeezing it so that there is no air in the tip. Never unroll the condom in advance. Hold the penis near the head in the other hand. (Be sure your man is aroused before clothing him in rubber.) Now place the rubber on the head and, curving your fingers slightly, unroll it and push it down. When carried out well, this can be a continuous flowing movement.

65 Oral condom wrap. Clamping the tip of the condom in your mouth, position it neatly over the head of his penis, then let the rim of your mouth unroll it down the shaft. Remember the trick of wrapping your lips across your teeth to avoid perforating the condom. This takes a bit of rehearsal.

66 Anything that gives your guy a novel sensation on his favorite body organ goes down well.

Try:

○ The acid from natural lemon juice or vodka

○ The tingle of minty toothpaste

○ The less stingy mint mouthwash

67 Process these in your own mouth first, and then lovingly apply them during oral sex.

hot tea AND
COLD ICE CUBES

68 Heat up the inside of your mouth first with a gulp of hot tea. Apply mouth to penis.

69 Enjoy for a minute, and then munch on an ice cube. As soon as possible, so that your man can be shocked by the contrast, apply mouth to penis again.

70 Take hot and cold in turns.

wash him WITH
GRITTY SKIN SCRUB

71 Coat your hands with a mild skin scrub. Hold his penis gently, and roll it backward and forward between your two hands.

72 At a later stage in the proceedings, slide the tip of one finger or two into his anus while operating on his penis either by hand or by mouth.

AYURVEDIC *honey bath*

73   The Ayurvedic massage treatment owes a great deal to the amazing sensation of warm oil being poured exquisitely all over you. In this variation, and only when swathed in towels or plastic sheeting, pour warmed (but not hot) melted honey over his genitals. The secret to the amazing sensation is to get a small but steady stream coming continuously. One way of doing this would be to put the honey in a sturdy plastic bag and pierce a small hole at the bottom.

74   Once the honey has coated his thighs, your task is to lick it off.

THE *sensuous* PENIS BATH

75 After all sensuous juices and substances have been rubbed in or licked off, it's time to bathe your man. Tell him that he is not to lift a finger. You are going to be his hand (and body) maiden. After you run the bath, ask him to sit on the edge with his feet in the bath water. Gently soap his genitals, paying attention to every nook and cranny.

76 When you have done as much as possible, ask him to sit down now in the bath and continue to stroke and clean his skin underwater.

77 Slide his foreskin back and clean underneath. Don't forget that soap can sting, so go easy on its use.

78 Don't forget that his perineum and anal passage will need attention too. Make your hand strokes like a slippery, slidy massage.

NEVER OVERLOOK
THE *impact* OF *underwear*

79   Underwear is intended to be seen and enjoyed by you and your man, so never remove clothes quickly (unless desperate, of course).

80   Sometimes it's exciting to wear a skirt just to let him see up it; it's not crude, but hot when a "nice" woman is deliberate about showing off her thighs.

81   Casually draw attention to your underwear—stand across the room from him, scantily clad, and get him to look from time to time. Don't forget to show him the back view.

82   As your underwear comes off, trail your stockings, etc., under his nostrils—and even wrap them round his throat. It's the small, in-your-face details that drive men wild.

PhD IN *penis pulling*

Did you know that the male orgasm contracts at 0.8 second intervals—exactly the same as that of the female? Time it.

83 Scarfing. If you've ever tried stimulating yourself through a layer of fine silk or chiffon, you'll understand the impact of this one. Wrap a flimsy scarf around your loved one's proud penis. With your hands on the scarfed area, use a gentle up-and-down motion, twisting occasionally. You can either move the skin under the scarf or you can move the scarf itself. Each offers a separate experience. Practice on your own fingers or genitals first to get the idea.

84 The jelly trick. This is for dedicated game players only. Fill a condom with as much sloppy jelly as it will hold, then fit it. Even though much of the jelly will be displaced, some will remain. Holding the condom tight at the top to contain the jelly, slide the other hand up and down his penis. Warm jelly offers a very different sensation than cold jelly.

85 The countdown. Pour on tons of lubricant. This penis massage consists of two strokes. First grip the top of the penis with the left hand and place the right hand underneath his testicles with the fingers pointing toward the anus. As you slide the left hand down, you bring the right hand up. You aim for them to meet somewhere around the base of the penis. The second stroke reverses this in that now you slide the left hand back up his penis and the right hand back down toward the anus. The key to a really sensual experience is to do the two strokes regularly and steadily. Then do the sequence ten times, then nine times, right down to one stroke only.

86 The pulsar. Clasp your two hands around the head of his penis. Squeeze gently, hold for a second, then let go. Pause. Then do it again. The trick is to imitate the rhythm of his pulse. When done during ejaculation, this can be fantastic. Time your pulsations to go with his contractions.

87 An occasional letdown is normal and should be ignored, especially on a first date or with an older man.

88 Says Bernadette, late thirties, from D.C.: "I've learned to roll over and switch to hands if he can manage a halfway erection that allows him to come. If not, I whisper, 'Do me instead.'"

89 Never turn lack of erection into a federal case unless he is rude or unpleasant. It can even mean he is too hot for you and your attractions.

90 Loss of erection in men under forty-five usually means they have become momentarily anxious or self-conscious. Go back a step—kiss and cuddle and get him to pleasure you. If you come on his hand, he will probably feel some return of confidence.

Old-time hooker tricks can also work, as we've said elsewhere:

91   Try a gentle finger in his anus.

92   Or pinch his nipples.

93   Or offer to let him do something "forbidden."

94   Or spank him.

95   Test his ability to delay orgasm by surrendering timing of the moment to you (a hugely pleasurable climax can eventually result).

THE *peaking* TRICK

96 When you sense your man is nearing his point of no return, stop genital stimulation for a while and focus on something else. Then go back to it. This is the concept of peaking. The more stopping and starting you do, the more peaking he will experience. The long-term benefit—his orgasm will be far more explosive.

97 With luck, you will be so tuned in to your partner that you will instinctively know what turns him on and what does not. But women can't always be mind readers (though they are pretty skillful). Sometimes your tricks will fall flat. Instead of taking this as a failure, tell yourself instead that you need more practice. So that you can get to know him better, you might ask him about:

○ His earliest sexual experiences.

○ His family memories of love and affection.

○ What he learned from the playground.

○ What he's learned as an adult.

○ His sexual failures.

○ His sexual successes.

Practice makes perfect!

three | TRICKS TO TEMPT AND TANTALIZE YOU

THE *clit* KIT

98 Make yourself a clit kit. Extraordinary former call girl Xaviera Hollander writes about what she describes as her survival package. She keeps alongside her bed:

○ A box of tissues

○ Lubricants for anal adventures and body anointing

○ Body lotion

○ Vaseline

○ Her contraceptive

○ Rubbers for him

○ A vibrator

○ A History of Western Philosophy (you can never know too much)

sensation
BOOSTERS

99   Consider wedging a vibrator next to your clitoris next time you make love. It works for both of you.

100   If you get too tense, bearing down (literally pushing out your genitals as in a bowel movement) helps to de-stress you.

101   If you reckon your vagina isn't getting enough sensation, cut down on the lubrication.

102   Did you know that Eastern women believe that a dry vagina gives their partner a better experience of intercourse?

103   If you are getting excited far too quickly, tell your partner you are dying to do oral sex on him and withdraw.

104   If you want to improve the strength of your orgasm, go for the stop-start method of "peaking."

105   If, during intercourse, you want to climax without masturbation, ask your man to help you.

106 If you adore combining masturbation with intercourse, however, enjoy, enjoy!

107 If you want to speed up orgasm, try clenching your buttocks, thighs, and vaginal muscles, then letting go, regularly.

108 A few women experience their first orgasm accidentally by leaning against the washing machine while it is working.

109 For a really sensational self-stimulation experience, try pulling down on your vagina from the rear while touching yourself at the front.

110 To heighten the rush you get from sex, try doing it with your head hanging over the side of the bed.

111 Sex trick: coat yourself liberally with massage oil before making love. This will allow you to slip and slide over and under your man.

Testosterone is the natural hormone that affects a woman's sex drive. Women who experience a sharp rise in sexual desire shortly before a period is due are likely to possess a high level of testosterone.

Women in the high testosterone range have the greatest levels of sexual arousal and maintain this arousal for the longest times. They also experience the highest frequencies of sexual fantasy.

Paradoxically, high-level testosterone women have less satisfactory love relationships than women with low testosterone.

An extra benefit to the high testosterone group: one study of fifty-two menopausal women showed that the high-testosterone group weighed an average of eighteen pounds less than the low-testosterone group.

High-testosterone women also had higher incomes!

Another study where single women were given testosterone replacement therapy showed that several dropped out, finding themselves unable to cope with their increased levels of sexual desire.

112 Women who find it difficult under normal circumstances to experience orgasm would be sensible to get a blood test to analyze their natural testosterone levels. If these are low, prescribed testosterone can improve:

○ sexual desire

○ sensitivity

○ experience of orgasm

113 If you want to make the most of your natural testosterone, use only barrier methods of birth control that do not interfere with your body's natural hormonal balance.

IMPROVE YOUR *climax*

The tension that leads up to orgasm is experienced all over the body. Climax itself relieves a lot of this, but a sudden cease-fire of sexual activity can leave a woman feeling strangely unsatisfied. You can improve your orgasmic ending after self-stimulation by:

114 Fitting your hand snugly down over your pubic mound with the fingers curved round inside the front of the vagina and simply pulling up against them. You do not slide your fingers but just exert a steady pressure.

115 If you like, actually throbbing your fingers in time with the remaining contractions. Some women find they can prolong their orgasm by deep pressing for many more contractions than they previously thought possible.

FAKING *orgasm*

116 Don't! It teaches people how NOT to satisfy you on a regular basis.

TELL IT *like it is*

Many of the suggestions in this section would also be well carried out by your lover. Remember, your lover cannot know what you personally like unless you tell him. He is not a mind reader. You need to find the courage and the technique to ask him to do the things that you love.

117 Preface your requests with praise: "I love the way you stimulate my clitoris. It's marvelous. Please, could you keep your hand firmly on my clitoris when I climax so that I can experience all of the climax."

118 When he concurs, tell him afterward, "That was the longest orgasm I've ever had." He'll soon get the hang of it!

119 Your man needs to know:

- If you like a soft or a firm touch.

- If you like your vagina stimulated.

- If you like your clitoris stimulated (who doesn't?).

- If you like your clitoris stimulated on the left side...

- Or the right side...

- Or on the head.

- If your perineum is sensitive.

- What you feel about penetration from the rear.

So let him hear it as it is.

BASIC *instinct*

Women with a high sex drive discover orgasm by basic instinct much as men do. But women with a medium or low sex drive may have to teach themselves. As many as 90 percent of women eventually reach orgasm by some means.

bliss FROM A
BOTTLE

120   Health food enthusiasts swear by ginseng.

121   Wine enthusiasts point out that two glasses of wine loosen inhibitions and make it easier to respond sexually.

sexy
CHECKLIST

You and your partner might like to:

122 Vary your lovemaking techniques.

123 Prolong your love sessions…

124 Or include more "quickies."

125 Use a personalized lubricant that becomes associated with your relationship.

126 Rent an X–rated video from the top shelf.

127 Visit a sex shop together.

128 Look at men's magazines; read mutual erotica.

129 Make love in unusual places, i.e. in the garden, on the roof, during a picnic in the woods.

130 Explore your G-spot.

131 See if you can bring him to orgasm by testicle stimulation alone.

style YOUR SHAPE

Using scissors and/or a razor, you might:

132 Remove most of your pubic hair, thus making yourself look much younger.

133 Style your pubic hair into a heart shape.

WOMAN,
know thyself

Get to know your clitoris as well as you know your face.

134 Check it out in the mirror.

135 Watch its color change as it gets increasingly excited.

136 Pull back your clitoral hood with one hand and gently touch the tip of the clitoris. It can feel much sexier done this way, plus you have the added advantage of not being able to lose the tip when it goes through one of its characteristic changes of size.

137 Check out a short up- and downstroke on the left side. Then compare this with the same on the right side.

138 Practice a light stroke, then a hard stroke.

139 Go for twirling on the clitoral head, then around the head.

G whiz

140 Your G-spot (if you have one—not every woman does) will be on the upper wall of the vagina probably a long way back. It helps if you (or your lover) possess long musician's fingers! The latest theory is that it is the clitoral root, the very base of the clitoris. Whatever! It feels like a small swelling.

THE *vaginal* PARTY

Your vagina is about to get a special celebration date. Make your bedroom private, warm, sweet-smelling, and comfortable. Your aim is to make your vagina feel wonderful.

141 Explore the outer rim by pulling down on it slightly with one finger. Most women find that the lower part of the vaginal entrance where it meets with the perineum feels sexiest.

142 Treat your perineum to a super vitamin E oil massage. This makes it supple and helps explore your particular sensitivities.

143 Try putting your longest fingers inside your vagina to find your G-spot.

144. To obtain sensuous feeling, press down on it with the pads of the finger(s), occasionally lightening then strengthening the pressure.

145. Push your left hand under your thigh and, coming up from underneath, put your forefingers in your vagina and pull backward until you can feel the area stretching back across the perineum. With your right hand, place your forefingers inside your vagina and pull it up toward the clitoris while your thumb gets busy on a very sensuous clitoral rub.

THUMBELINA

Let rip with a little thumb work on the erogenous zones.

146 Use the thumbs to twirl around the nipples.

147 Then twirl at the far side of each breast.

148 Then up and down the sides of the breasts.

149 Tucking your hand below your perineum, stroke with the fingers while using your thumb to move rhythmically against the clitoris. It feels like two people making love to you.

four | TURN UP
THE HEAT

EROTIC
piercing

150   If you're brave and willing to go for a dramatic alteration, consider piercing. The look can be exotic and wildly sexy. Devotees of erotic piercing insist that the piercing itself is an erotic event to be shared with the friend of your heart. What's more, those rings and studs make for spectacular sensation during sex. Prime erotic sites are:

○ The nipples

○ The navel

○ The labia

tricks
YOU CAN TURN

151 In the red museum. You are an exhibit and your dream partner is blindfolded. He has to identify you through caressing your naked body, and you cannot move, regardless of where he touches.

152 The seven veils. A beautiful slave is brought to the auction block swathed in cloaks and scarves. The cruel slave master slowly peels these away as he describes exactly what he plans to do to the slave. Beneath the cloaks are many thin veils. For each veil that is ripped off, the slave is ravished in some manner.

153 Butterfly kisses. You are naked and forced to lie down in a garden full of flowers. Next you are blindfolded and your erogenous zones painted with a syrup and water mixture that attracts butterflies. Now you have to guess whether it is your partner or a butterfly who touches you. For every wrong guess, you are lightly chastised. But with each wrong guess, the chastisement gets tougher!

154 Star stripper. On a clear night, you go out to view the stars. When you return indoors, you must identify ten of the constellations you have just seen. For each mistake, you must do something scintillating and starry to your partner.

155 The photographic model. Your poses get more and more extreme until finally you are forced to have sex with the photographer "for the sake of art." See the Antonioni film *Blowup* for inspiration.

156 The high-class hooker. You ask your client to tell you exactly what he wants you to do to him. Every time you finish one activity, you must ask for the next command. You continue until one of you can go no farther.

157 The detective trail. Invite your partner over and leave a trail of clues (such as a red rose, a black condom, a lacy bra) so that he ultimately finds his way into your chamber.

158 In Transylvania. He is the vampire, and you are the victim. His task is to seriously arouse you by making love to your neck only. He is allowed to suck, nip, lick, tickle, breathe, manipulate your head and neck, and thoroughly restrain your body. (Biting by negotiation only.)

159 Fair exchange. He is allowed to make love exclusively to your breasts, provided you are allowed to make love exclusively to his buttocks and back. You each take a turn for the other and accept whatever the other chooses to dish out—including orgasm.

160 Torture by tickling. Literally what it sounds like. Bind your partner (loosely) to the bed; then target his most sensitive areas. Ensure that your touch is extremely light and moves rapidly, like a spider darting.

Most ticklish areas:

○ Feet

○ Belly

○ Armpits

○ Inner thighs

○ Around the chest

161 Play at pornographers. If you have your own video camera, make your own "blue" movie. Then watch it together from your bed. A word of warning: if there is any likelihood your partner is not trustworthy, don't do it. Intimate photos have been known to show up on people's computers on the other side of the world.

162 The quickest. Time your partner (stopwatch in hand) to see how fast he can race to climax. Then take your own turn. Give the winner a prize.

163 The slowest. Time your partner (stopwatch again) and see how many hours sex can be dragged out for. Then take your own turn. The prize here is a good sleep.

164 Erotic postcards. Document your love affair with shots of your sexiest moments, but make sure neither of you can be identified in the pictures. The challenge is to invent the sexiest postcard to be carried safely in your bag.

165 Erotic reading. There are two excellent websites that provide high-quality erotic stories mainly, but not exclusively, for women. These are www.erotica-readers.com and www.cleansheets.com.

166 Please Daddy, tell me a story. Reading aloud in bed is an erotic art, presently undervalued. A ten- or fifteen-minute story with a romantic/erotic build-up can feel scintillating. Look in the back of our book, *How to Make Great Love to a Woman*, for short-story material.

167 Show me a movie. Going to bed with your television set has a lot to be said for it. A really sexy movie like *9 1/2 Weeks* or *Betty Blue* can sometimes get so exciting you find you have missed the end of the film.

168 Hello Mom. Sneak up on your fellow while he is talking on the phone to his mother and give him a surprise erection. He'll either love you or kill you.

169 Sitting in the backseat. Drive out to a secluded place where you cannot be seen or found by anyone and move to the back seat. In spite of the inconvenience and the cramps, the sheer unfamiliarity of the surroundings gets you moving at up to 100 mph.

170 Spread a plastic sheet across the carpet, cover each other's bodies in melted chocolate, and see who can lick the most off first. Best quality chocolate only. Prize? A choco-orgasm.

be A MAN

Agree with your partner that you and he will change sex for the day. This involves:

171   Dressing in opposite-sex clothing.

172   Switching gender roles. Think yourself into character and act as it feels appropriate. Women sometimes become amazingly pushy and men surprisingly meek.

getting RAUNCHIER

173 The joy of shoes. Did you know that one of the real sex differences between men and women is that men get turned on by what they see? This is why they only have to glance at a pair of high heels to get hard. So even if it ruins you, invest in a pair of gorgeous, spindly Manolo Blahniks—*Sex and the City* style.

174 Stockings too, preferably with seams, add to the illusion of flawless but flashy legs. So next time you come out of the bathroom, keep on your lingerie, stockings, and heels, and ask your man to roll onto his belly. Then walk up and down his body, taking care to keep your weight off his spine. Make sure he can see what is happening in a floor-length mirror.

175 Experiment with implements—there are usually several in the kitchen drawer—made of wood.

176 Play the dice game to see who is in charge for the night—the first one to throw a six is boss.

177 Find out how far he likes to lace his pain with pleasure; clothespins make effective nipple clamps.

178 Mouth appeal. The glossy, pulpy look of luscious lips puts the erotically sensitive male in immediate mind of your other lips—the hidden part of your anatomy. Let him see your mouth stretch and smile. And Grub Smith, author of *Real Sex*, insists that a pointed tongue, especially when it happens to be licking a penis, is one of the sexiest sights ever!

179 A rubber erection. Sexual pioneer Tuppy Owens of The Outsiders Club has devised The Rubber Wall, which she erects at her famous Sex Maniac's Ball, an annual event in the U.K. The Rubber Wall is a large sheet of translucent, back-lit rubber, which you can dance against and slither around, moving against bodies doing the same thing on the other side. You might erect your own Rubber Wall, and with a copious supply of glistening, gleaming oil, tell your man that as he gyrates on his side, several women will be pressing up against him on the other side. Now it's your chance to break out into multiple personalities.

WHO WANTS TO BE
AN *exhibitionist?*

180 Recline on a bed in front of large mirror.

181 Look at yourself in the mirror as you begin to touch your labia and vulva. Watch your face as well as your hands. Watch your arousal build.

182 If you want to thrust, do so. Don't act to the mirror. But exaggerate your movements—it will turn you on more.

183 Invite your partner to watch.

184 Invite your partner to take part.

185 Dress up for your mirror. Oil your body. Groom your man. Tell yourselves you are doing this for a live sex show.

186 Enjoy, enjoy!

NO *bullshit*

187 Although it's true that all these sex tricks can turn your man on, their impact also depends on your state of mind. If you are dressing and acting sexy because your man turns you on like nothing else, that's great. There's nothing quite like the exchange of incredible sexual attraction. If, on the other hand, you don't really like the man you are manipulating, it shows. And although he may be attracted, if you are not, what is the point? Never function on automatic.

five

VIBES, LUBES, AND SEX TOYS

VIBES— *THE very latest models*

There's a small revolution going on in the sex-toys industry. Vibrators are being transformed as a result of the fabulous new materials now available. They are soft, malleable, feel like real skin in fun materials such as see-through translucent jellies, and are in gorgeous jewel-like colors. Here are some of the best, many of which can be found on the top vibrator website on the Internet— www.goodvibes.com.

188 The Hitachi Magic Wand is still the Rolls-Royce of vibrators, and is still a bestseller. This enormous two-speed plug-in model possesses a sturdy wand handle and a huge vibrating head. What is new about it is that there are now attachments fitting onto the head that focus on clitoral stimulation.

189 Acuvibe. This is similar to the Magic Wand but with rechargeable batteries which last for a good twenty minutes. If you hate all those trailing wires, this is the model for you.

190 Tech Rabbit. This is an improved version of all those other rabbits and a bestseller for Passion8.co.uk.

191 Attachments. What is special about the last two vibrators is that there are some cute pink or purple G-spot attachments that can also be used to give your guy a prostate massage. One has a slender curved tip specially shaped to give maximum pressure on the front wall of the vagina where the mysterious female G-spot is located.

192 Relaxus Rechargeable. This is the most powerful battery vibrator of the lot. What's more, the rechargeable batteries last for sixty minutes. If you get off on a really intense stimulation, this is the one.

193 Coil-operated vibrators. These are the more old-fashioned shapes that look a bit like unwieldy handguns. The Wahl possesses the great advantage of being much quieter than most other large vibrators.

194 Most of the older vibrators are still fast, intense, and effective. But watch the battery! One 1970s calculation had it that there is a maximum oscillation (vibration) speed needed for women to be able to reach orgasm. This means that if a vibrator's battery is wearing down, you may suddenly find it much more difficult to come.

vibes YOU MIGHT LIKE TO BUY *him*

195 Ecsta-Sleeve Vulva. A stretchable sleeve made of cyberskin that fits over the penis and includes a vibrating egg for stimulating the sensitive head of the penis.

196 The Screaming O Vibrating Ring. It's exceptional in that it's disposable. It slips downs to the base of the penis, fits snugly, and provides a mild vibration that lasts for around thirty minutes. Made of translucent coral silicone with a sensational beaded edge, it stretches to fit. Its mild vibratory effect is surprisingly helpful to appreciative female partners.

197 Neptune Ring Vibe. This is a tiny vibrating dolphin attached to a cock ring. This works either by giving your lover a solo buzz or by stimulating your clitoris during intercourse.

198 The Big O is a cock ring with a staggering nine-stage vibration pattern, providing both pulses and intensity changes to suit your particular pleasure. Made of translucent coral silicone, it stretches up to five inches!

199 Natural Contours. These are small nonphallic-shaped vibrators designed by women's soft-porn filmmaker Candida Royale after she got thoroughly fed up with the design of the old-fashioned male-inspired sort. They look like objets d'art in candy colors and are small enough to fit into the contours of your hand. Your great aunt might never know what they are for!

pulsating VIBRATORS

Recent improvements in vibrator design take into account the great significance of stimulating the G-spot as well as the clitoris. The shape and fit of vibrators have been modified so that they provide not only friction, but also pulsation.

200 The Astro Vibe is thick and phallic. It comes in sinister black with a generous white head, and it's made of soft, skin-friendly ThermoPlastic Elastomer. It sends powerful vibrations from the disc switch control to the tilted head, which has been specifically designed to hit the G-spot better.

201 The Onye vibrator is one of the best pulsating vibrators around. It looks like a neat shiny, black cylinder, rounded at both ends, and it's small enough to be used as a travel accessory. It has a mind-blowing eight speeds of vibration and five separate and different pulsation patterns.

202 Pretty in Pink is phallic shaped but consists of a series of graduated beads, with the largest at the bottom tapering off to the smallest. Made of pink jelly rubber, it is soft. And firm. And very quiet.

203 The Aqua Rabbit is a version of the sensational Rabbit vibrators, but this one is safe to use in the bath or in the shower. It's made of lavender-colored gel and looks delicious—good enough to eat.

204 Laya is a quick, multispeed, hypoallergenic vibrator designed to hug the clitoral area. It actually cups the entire vulva and feels wonderful. It's neat, lightweight, and fits into a handbag. It's perfect for those who may be allergic to other rubber products.

The ancient Japanese considered it taboo to make sex toys resembling human genitals, so dildos were carved to resemble other living creatures. This tradition has lasted through to the modern version of the dildo—the vibrator.

205 Fukuoku 9000 is one of the most ingenious newer vibrators. Working off tiny watch batteries, it fits over your finger like a tiny finger sheath and vibrates. There is no battery pack and no cord. Perfect for surprises during intercourse since it is virtually undetectable. The kit includes textured rubber pads to fit over the device so that you can vary your finger sensation.

206 Pocket Rocket is a small rocket-shaped vibrator—a little like a pocket flashlight in appearance. But what transforms it are the wonderful jelly rubber sleeves that fit over it. Comes in lustrous, edible colors such as blueberry, grape, lime, strawberry, and tangerine.

207 The famous Rabbit Pearl. This consists of a rabbit head (with extra long ears!) and a midsection of tumbling pearls or a variety of nubbly textures that create a unique scintillating sensation against the walls of the vagina at the same time that the rabbit ears flutter the clitoris. Made of translucent pink vinyl.

208 Silver Pearl. This has a sci-fi appearance with a rotating shaft and strong clitoral probe. The silver pearls in the middle speed along a track to provide a rolling sensation in the vagina. Controls are on a lighted display so that you can adjust in the dark!

209 Mini Tongue Vibe looks like a flesh-colored tongue protruding from a silver-colored base. With three speeds, all you have to do is close your eyes and imagine that there is the most versatile of lovers lapping away and giving you thrilling oral sex.

A *round peg* IN A...

210 Have you ever felt uncomfortable in a sex shop or felt they were very male-oriented? You can search the Internet for any number of sex boutiques and find those especially designed for women. Strap-on dildos are best-selling items, as well as a variety of anal toys.

butt PLUGS

211 Butt plugs are designed to be worn for the feeling of fullness. They are made in silicone or rubber and are easy to clean. Some butt plugs come with heart-shaped bases, and the silicone is excellent for transmitting vibrations—all you have to do is apply your vibrator to the base. These plugs come in a variety of shapes and sizes. There is:

○ The long, thin, pointed plug

○ The shorter, fatter, slightly curved version

○ The small, squat, fat-beaded version

anal GAMES

212 Thai beads. A string of three small, pearly pink beads to be inserted into the anus and then pulled out slowly to accentuate stimulation or in a rush for a thundering climax.

213 Jumbo beads. A graduated larger version.

214 Jelly beads. Spongy, ruby-colored, equally sized jelly beads with a ring pull that offers a jelly-like sensation.

HANDS *free*

215 The double delight. A variety of two-ended dildos to be worn either between women or between heterosexuals when the man enjoys anal penetration.

216 The scissor dildo is a double dildo shaped like a pair of scissors that enables you to penetrate your partner with particular flexibility.

217 The mini-hummer offers targeted vibration for women who find it hard to come. You wear it strapped in place over your clitoris, held on by an elastic waist strap and leg straps. Can be worn during intercourse.

218 Venus Penis. This is a curved jelly butterfly shape with an integrated dildo so that you can enjoy a spot of penetration as your buzzer stimulates your clitoris.

219 Triple Stimulation. This is a cock ring with a flexible dildo for anal penetration while your man is also penetrating your vagina.

LUBES

Passion8 is a particularly well run and discreet sex-toy supplier which operates entirely by mail order. The lubes it sells are the wettest and juiciest. All of these lubricants can be bought from Passion8 (www.passion8.co.uk), www.condomania.com, or www.condomsdirect.co.uk

220 Sylk. Tasteless, odorless, and non-greasy, Sylk mimics the natural vaginal juices. A free sachet is available for sampling. Especially important, Sylk is safe to be used with condoms.

221 K-Y Jelly. That great old stand-by. It's excellent for use with sex toys and pelvic exercises, but NOT to be used with condoms.

222 Wet Platinum. This is a top quality U.S. lubricant made by Dr. Johnson. It comes in a sexy black bottle and stays wetter and slipperier for longer than any other lubricant in clinical trials. For use by men and women, it's oil free and may be used with condoms.

223 Durex Play Warmer and Durex Play Tingling. The former provides a warm sensation, and the tingle gets you tingling in exactly the right places.

224 Sensilube. Made by Durex especially for women with lubrication problems. This is my own personal choice, not least because you can buy it over the counter at any good pharmacist.

fun LUBES

Lubricants come in dozens of flavors and colors. Try:

225 Edible lubes, small gelatin-filled capsules that you bite on during oral sex to flood your partner's genitals with sweet-smelling edible gel...

226 Or chocolate-flavored gel...

227 Or a row of little gelatin pots for flexibility of selection.

228 There are so many different kinds that you are best advised to search two main sites for suggestions. Go to www.annsummers.com or www.goodvibes.com. You can use lubes to spice up the greatest blow job of your man's entire life or to flood in your vagina at the moment of penetration.

229 Trick: if you are vaginally dry, please don't lose sight of the fact that this may mean you are not feeling emotionally safe with your partner. This means that you would be wise to work on making the relationship more intimate before going on to sex.

230 These days it's getting positively normal to spice up the bedroom with toys. Ann Summers, the British high-street sex-shop chain, suggests:

- Handcuffs, in black leather or pink and fluffy

- Self-adhesive diamanté tattoos

- PVC blindfold

- Kinky heart-shaped bottom paddle

- Fur collar and lead

- Nipple chain

restrain yourself
PLEASE

231 Look online for any number of sinister-looking restraints. Several U.S. erotica companies revealed that nipple clamps have been top bestsellers.

Favorite restraint equipment includes:

○ Whips

○ Canes

○ Paddles

○ Cat o' nine tails

○ Tackle for tying your partner to the bed or padlocking him to the furniture

SEXUAL *electricity*

There's the emotional electricity that sparks between you and your man. But there's also the sort that uses Faraday electricity and bombards him with safe, low-voltage, mini-lightning bolts. Many of you will have heard of TENS machines, small box-like objects used in physiotherapy, which, by pulsating a tiny electrical charge into the skin, relieve physical pain.

232 Now there is a sexual version of a TENS machine called the Violet Wand. It's been on sale since the 1930s and is presently enjoying a resurrection of interest. It operates by sending sparks through a single electrode and creates an incredible array of sensations. When held near your body, it sends out a continuous stream of tiny lightning bolts and gives off a distinct purple light.

233 Try kissing while plugged in—better than any spark from a hotel carpet!

234 Available from www.stockroom.com are several sex toys (including the Violet Wand) that use the Faraday principle. There are electrical:

○ Butt plugs

○ Cock rings

○ Vaginal shields

235 Lovemaking in the missionary position while simultaneously using a Violet Wand brings a whole new spark of enthusiasm to an old classic!

SOMETHING FOR *madame*

Skin Two (www.skintwo.com) makes exceptional clothes out of rubber and PVC. They are slick, shiny, and skintight. They are also beautifully cut, immensely flattering, and stunningly erotic.

The PVC comes in several new textures. As well as the original PVC, there is a realistic leather-look, a matte version like unpolished rubber, snakeskin, and a slinky, sensational satin finish. Try any or all of these:

236 Gorgeous basques and bodysuits.

237 Catsuits and dresses with keyhole cutouts over the breasts.

238 Shiny, glossy military dress and maid, nurse, and dominatrix dresses, all in glorious shiny, shimmering rubber or PVC.

GETTING
six YOURSELF
IN THE MOOD

kundalini MEDITATION

Practitioners of kundalini yoga use a special "opening-up-the-body meditation" before meeting their lovers. The meditation is divided into four parts. To try it, you can:

239 Stand in one spot, with your knees bent. Let your whole body shake so that it lets go of any tension you might be feeling.

240 Put on some music and dance, letting your body flow naturally to the rhythms.

241 Sit and watch your mind at work, as if it were a film and you were viewing it.

242 Lie down and sense the support that the ground offers you.

243 Go bathing. Arrange open-ended time when you can luxuriate in a sweet-scented bath surrounded by glowing wax night lights, with sensual music playing. Privacy is important. Luxuriously soap yourself with the latest exotic moisturizer, and let your hands glide over your slippery body. Don't forget to include your genitals, and spend as long as you like, provided you remain warm.

244 When you emerge from the bath water, using one of the new intensive Ayurvedic oils, anoint your body lightly, omitting only the genitals.

245 See www.momentum98.com or www.nyrusa.com for a wonderful supply of natural flower fragrances with safe, healthy oil bases.

246 Make your bedroom a pleasure dome. Treat yourself like an honored guest. Prepare your bedroom so that it is clean and tidy, lit with scented candles (as many or as few as you like), warm, and comfortable. Place some flowers where your eyes can easily fall on them. Above all, arrange some warm, fluffy toweling on the bed and place by the side of the bed your massage oil, a packet of tissues, and your favorite sex toys. Your aim is to enhance the atmosphere, visually and tactilely.

247 Search out your hot spots. Your pleasurable task is to touch and tantalize all areas of your body and register your own particular hot spots. Every woman is different. Every woman's eroticism is personal to her and unique. Where one person may get incredibly hot from having her nipples tweaked, others get the sensual shakes from walking spider fingers across the lower abdomen.

248 Pleasure yourself. You think so highly of yourself that you are prepared to make yourself the gift of an hour's precious time. During that time you are going to pamper your body with the most sensational selfmassage you have ever enjoyed. You are a queen who is entitled to body pampering. You slip and slide and glide over every seam and nook in your soft and creamy skin. You are going to touch:

○ Your face

○ Your chest

○ Your abdomen

○ Your genitals

○ Your legs

○ Your feet

249 Tactile trick: experiment with grades of touch, from quite hard to fairy light.

250 Hottest spot of the lot. Although we vary in our type of response to clitoral stimulation, most of us would agree that this is the sexual power station. Your task now is to experiment with the sort of sensation that your clitoris enjoys. Just as you have searched out the erogenous zones on the rest of the body, now you not only locate your pleasure places, but you are encouraged to build on the sensations you find here. Once more experiment with different pressures.

251 Tactile trick: many women say that the area to the left of their clitoris (as they look down) is the most sensational.

252 Know your clitoral tip. Is it small or large? Is it easy to view or hidden away in the folds? Does it get erect easily, or does it take time before it slowly responds?

253 Take a look at it in the mirror. Pull the pubic mound above it right back to expose it. Try the trick of stimulating it while watching yourself in the mirror. Do your genitals change color as you get aroused? When you get ultra excited, does it strangely seem to disappear? Follow it through as it sinks back into your engorged labia. Keep on stroking. When you have climaxed, watch what happens to your clitoris in the mirror.

254 Know your anus. If you are brought up in the UK or the U.S., you have probably been taught that the anal opening is dirty and basically a taboo area. Mainland Europeans, however, have a more realistic attitude. They are used to regular bathing (in bidets), inserting gelatin suppositories to aid excretion, and even taking the temperature with a rectal thermometer. It's good to reach this degree of comfort with your anus so that you can feel emotionally free to include anal stimulation with great sex. How could you stimulate it?

255 Bathe it.

256 Stroke it.

257 Rub your finger around the outer rim.

258 Stretch that outer rim a little.

259 Slip your finger a little way inside and push. Try to enlarge the opening slightly.

260 Push "around the clock face"—on the hour, quarter, half, and three-quarters position. Each provides a different sensation.

261 Know your orgasm. Include anal stimulation with one hand (from underneath) while you focus on clitoral stimulation with the other. You are likely to find that the anal stimulation heightens excitement and turns you on.

262 Don't let yourself come too quickly. If you sense you are about to climax, halt the sensation for a short time. This delays proceedings and allows you to grow even more aroused next time. This sequence of stimulating then stopping as you near orgasm is called "peaking."

263 Orgasm options: how many different sorts of orgasm can you have? There are short ones and shallow ones, long ones and intense ones. There are orgasms that barely ripple, and orgasms that cause a cataclysm. What's more, one person may be capable of feeling not just different lengths and strengths of sensation, but may also experience orgasm in several different sites in the body simultaneously.

daring DECISIONS

264 If a feeling of fullness is vital to your experience of a really fantastic orgasm, consider investing in:

○ A large dildo or vibrator.

○ A butt plug. (Buy the correct size for your level of elasticity.)

○ One of the Japanese double or triple vibrators where just about every orifice you can think of is thoroughly stimulated.

265 Germaine Greer's words of wisdom: Australian feminist Germaine Greer wrote a famous book in the late 1960s called ***The Female Eunuch***. One of its most daring (and meaningful lines) was: "If you haven't ever tasted your own menstrual flow, then sister, you haven't lived!" Think about it. You expect your man to be comfortable with your bodily juices. But don't you think you should be comfortable, too? Tricky but true.

FANTASIES, *fantasies*

You can try every sex position you can think of, including dangling from the ceiling, but if you don't bring your fertile brain into play, you may not manage to become aroused. The brain plays a surprisingly large part in getting aroused. Long after the sex hormones have quit the body of the older woman, her imagination is still capable of arousing and bringing her back to climax.

If thinking of your present lover doesn't quite do it, you might consider dreaming of:

266 The juiciest movie star you can think of.

267 Being the temple victim inseminated by the sinister warlock.

268 Ravishing a beautiful young man in the woods.

269 Riding a powerful motorbike that heats and vibrates between your legs.

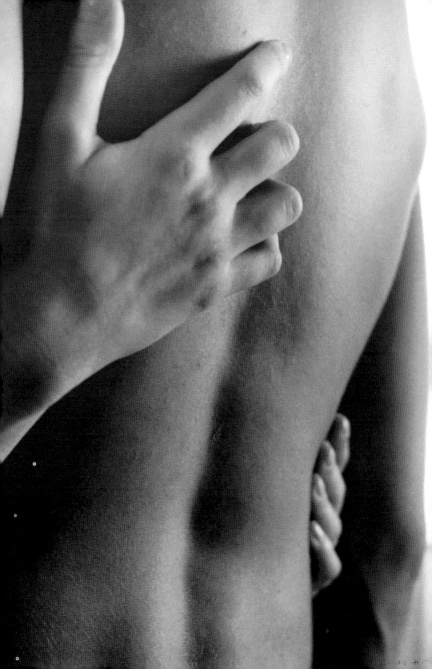